Élisabeth Hardouin-Fugier

FOURVIÈRE
The story behind the basilica

LA TAILLANDERIE

PLURIELS

"PLURIELS" COLLECTION

Directed by Gérald Gambier

Text:
Elisabeth Hardouin-Fugier

Photographs:
- **Gérald Gambier**
- **Corinne Janier:**
pages 28 and 29

Graphics and maps:
Corinne Janier

Translation:
Office Européen de Communication

Contents

© Éditions La Taillanderie · 2006
rue des Frères-Lumière
01400 Châtillon-sur-Chalaronne
Tél : 04 74 55 16 59
Fax : 04 74 55 14 27
contact@la-taillanderie.com
www.la-taillanderie.com
ISBN 2-87629-355-2
ISSN en cours

MERCI MARIE

During the four days of the Festival of Lights, the basilica shines brightly over the city. This is the most spectacular work of Lyon's lighting designers, now famous the world over for their art and expertise.

The imposing mass of Fourvière Basilica rises into the wide Lyon sky, as if in response to the Alpine peaks in the distant east. 2000 years earlier, Roman architects had also sought to make their mark on the immense Lyon sky by building a colossal forum. For many centuries, it remained the largest structure on the hill because wine-growing was preferred to building. Since the end of the 19th century, the monumental church dedicated to the Virgin Mary has stood as a landmark, visible from far and wide. The third millennium, with its skyscrapers, motorways and radio relay towers, is humbled by this symbol of a worldwide culture.

ALWAYS A GIFT

LITTLE FREE LIBRARY

NEVER FOR SALE

Bossan's construction makes a strong mark on the Lyon skyline, but some traces of the past remain.

Four towers for Mary, one for Eiffel

Fourvière Basilica dominates Lyon in the same way Montmartre dominates Paris. Both churches were born of pious promises made as the Prussian Army advanced on France. In Lyon, on 8 October 1870, Monsignor Ginouilhac pledged in the name of all Catholics to build a church on Fourvière hill, dedicated to Mary, if Lyon were spared the invading army. When the "miracle" occurred, it was a moment to celebrate the Virgin and to build a high golden basilica in honour of Her glory and the true faith.

Tower 1889
Bourdon 1919

Saint Michael
Millefaut 1885

Public observatory 1881

Golden Virgin
Fabisch 1852

Bell tower
Duboys 1851

13 bells 1891

Porte des Lions
1876

Saint Thomas
Chapel

Local Catholics upheld their promise to Mary, in spite of a hefty price tag: 2 million gold francs to build the church designed by architect Pierre Bossan. At Montmartre, though the money flowed in quickly, it was felt that the church should be austere, in keeping with the solemnity of the promise made to Mary.

As for Lyon's free-thinkers, partisans of the Republic or mere citizens with little church-going fervour, they saw the opulence and monumental size of the basilica as a provocation. The City Councilmen spoke of Fourvière as a "citadel of superstition... an insolent defiance of local democracy." In 1882, Guignol, a beloved Lyon puppet character, took sides with Mary of the humble people, but against the "Lords of Fourvière" and their delusions of grandeur. A war of words raged in the local press.

In Lameire's mosaic, "The Arrival of Saint Pothin", the artist symbolically represented the successors of the Apostles.

In the mosaic of the Vow of Louis XIII, we see the most prestigious churches of various eras, for example Montmartre, which appears between the cathedrals of Chartres and Paris, with angels flying overhead.

From their 48.5 metre perch, the towers and the statue of Saint Michael appear invincible. But the World Fair of 1894, held in Lyon, was seen as something of an anticlerical revenge. An Eiffel tower was built next to the church, rising tens of metres higher than the Virgin, as a clear reminder of the Parisian monument, built to commemorate the 100th anniversary of the French Revolution.

In about 1938, enamelled advertising plates were mounted in the tramways, showing the two monuments on the hill, and the store name "Grande Pharmacie Lyonnaise." The logo has been somewhat modernised but still exists today.

And yet these two competing symbols were both immediately accepted into the local landscape. They even appeared side by side in an advertisement banner of the Grande Pharmacie Lyonnaise, vying for space on the Lyon skyline.

A replica of the Eiffel Tower in Paris, this 80-metre tower was erected during the World Fair in Lyon in 1894. The metal tower once stood on a Moorish style base.

Fourvière Hill, a witness to the past

Fourvière's prestigious past sets it apart from churches such as Lourdes and La Salette, built following miraculous apparitions of the Virgin in remote mountain areas. In Lyon, Roman antiquity continues to be felt not only in the numerous vestiges, but also in the local vocabulary: first, there is the name Fourvière, from forum, transformed over the centuries to Fore Vetus, Forverium, Forvere, Forvières, and Fourvières. Circa 58 BC, Julius Cesar set up a military base here of 30,000 men; in 43 BC, his lieutenant, Munatius Plancus, founded the town of Lugdunum, later dominated by the grandiose constructions of Hadrian (117-138 AD). The Lameire mosaic, The Arrival of Saint Pothin in Lyon, gives us an idea of the Roman heydays. The basilica was built on a retaining wall of the vast forum which had

The Roman forum, in the centre of the mosaic of Saint Pothin, is a work of the architect A.M. Chenavard.

The bell tower by Duboys in 1851, built by order of Cardinal de Bonald.

collapsed in the year 840. Some of the stone blocks of the forum can be seen in the Rosaire gardens. Legend tells us that worship of the Virgin supplanted worship of Roman goddesses. Legend incorrectly tells us that the martyrdom of Lyon's Christians in 177 took place at the amphitheatre of Fourvière.

Archaeological digs on the Roman site began in 1887, and soon revealed its very rich past. Under the glacial moraine, a crystalline base made it possible to build a bridge on the Saône River in the 11th century, which encouraged the construction of housing and the reconstruction of Saint-Jean Cathedral, in the new Gothic style, under the aegis of Archbishop Guichard, who had welcomed the exiled Archbishop of Canterbury, Thomas Becket. In 1168, a modest little chapel dedicated to the Virgin was built on Fourvière Hill, by order of Olivier de Chavannes, dean of the cathedral. In 1170, after the Archbishop of Canterbury was assassinated in his cathedral, the nave of the chapel was expanded, in memory of this new martyr, canonised in 1173. The English archbishop, Jean Bellesmains, gave

the Fourvière chapel a Canon chapter in 1192, under the authority of the cathedral which, for three centuries, experienced various difficulties, detailed in the Acts-Capitular. The small chapel with its two parallel naves worshiped Saint Thomas Becket rather more than the Virgin. Fourvière did not greatly benefit from the two important councils in 1245 and 1274, though they designated Lyon as the "second Rome."

Fourvière was caught up in a series of political troubles, from the revolt of Lyon against the authority of the cathedral chapter in 1269, to the pillages of the Tard-Venus. When the city of Lyon came into the French fold, under Charles V, the king allowed the city to build fortifications including Fourvière in its territory. The chapel tower became a lookout post for guards controlling the gates to the city. The Fourvière pilgrimage had to compete with that of the miraculous Virgin of Ile Barbe and especially that of Notre-Dame de France, in Puy-en-Velay, on the Compostela trail. Neither the flourishing economy of Lyon, at its height in the Renaissance, nor its ecclesiastic prestige did much good for Fourvière: after the pillaging by the Protestant armies (1562), the chapel was merely rebuilt much as it had been.

Many souvenir engravings were sold to pilgrims, including this image of the statue of Mary known as Notre-Dame de Fourvières. Until the end of the 19th century, Fourvière was written with a final "s".

After the construction of the nave by Delamonce, two portals with different frontons gave access to the two parallel naves. The one on the left is dedicated to Saint Thomas Becket, the other opens onto the more recent nave.

Only a few column capitals remain from the medieval period, which saw little activity in Fourvière. References to antiquity were still strong and the consecration of 1872 mentions that the new church was built on the site of the old Roman forum.

Lyon looks to Mary

Veneration of the Virgin grew steadily, as can be seen in the visit by Louis XI, come to pray to Notre-Dame du Bon-Conseil, followed by Anne of Austria, praying to have a child. Shortly after his trip through Lyon, Louis XIII dedicated France to the Virgin in a ceremony which is depicted in the mosaic The Vow of Louis XIII.

The people of Lyon have regularly called on Mary for protection. The town authorities made vows in exchange for keeping the city safe from various epidemics. The Rectors of the Aumône-Générale, in charge of the Civil Hospices, prayed for orphans to be spared the ravages of scabies; the Échevins (town councillors) prayed in 1643 for protection against the plague. This particular vow is represented in a stained glass window

The retable at the end of the Delamonce nave is typical of the baroque opulence in vogue at the time.

The ex-voto promised during the bombings of 1793 is one of the rare survivors of the Revolutionary period.

by Bégule. Still today, every September 8th, the City of Lyon makes an offering to the ecclesiastic authorities at Fourvière.

Worship of the Virgin Mary spread throughout Lyon. The provost of merchants paid for a statue on Pont du Change, and another in front of the stock exchange. Hundreds of statues were erected at street corners, including the famous Virgin by Coysevox (1697). A brotherhood was organised by Monsignor de Neuville, who blessed the city every Saturday, from a window at Fourvière, with his ostensorium and consecrated wafer. This typical rite is performed every September 8th by the Cardinal of Lyon, from a special gallery in the basilica. The name Notre-Dame des Grâces appears in the painting on an altar by Claude Ferrier. Lyon silk makers offered robes to two venerated statues of Mary, Notre- Dame des Grâces and Notre-Dame du Bon-Conseil.

In the 18th century, vows were made during immense processions. To accommodate the crowds, the architect Delamonce proposed several plans, but built only one, the nave, in 1740. One of the oldest statues, known as Notre-Dame de Fourvières, reigns from the centre of a golden rococo decor, surrounded by votive hearts and ex-voto in thanks for her many mercies.

page 11 : The Vow of the Échevins in 1643. Stained glass window by Lucien Bégule, former chapel of Fourvière, 1882.

NOTRE...
DE FO...

VOEV
DES ECHEVINS

Colour wash attributed to Grobon, representing the old chapel in the 19th century.

Orsel was commissioned to paint this allegory during the cholera epidemic of 1832. It was completed in 1852 by his students, who added a view of Fourvière in 1832. The City of Lyon, kneeling, and a wounded lion implore the Virgin, surrounded by the patron saints of Lyon (John the Baptist, Pothin, Irénée, Blandine), to send her angels to chase away the epidemic.

Around the church, large buildings made of a clay and straw mix housed the clerics. On the "Hill that Prays", gardening was a favourite occupation. A meticulous surveyor, Chevalard, drew the plans for the grounds and vineyards of the church, but the tranquillity of the site was soon disturbed by the Revolution.

In 1793, Fourvière was sold as a National Asset. During the siege of Lyon, the clerics looked on as the armies of the Convention fired on the Hôtel-Dieu. The Ladies of Hôtel-Dieu made the solemn promise to offer an ex-voto painting telling of the miraculous rescue of the patients.

Fourvière chapel was reopened by Pope Pius VII, on his return from the crowning of Napoleon in Paris (19 April 1805) and the pilgrimage was renewed, thanks to the support of Napoleon's nephew, Cardinal Fesch, who was Archbishop of Lyon at the time. Votive processions were a regular event in the city, organised by leading figures such as the Duchess of Orleans and Maréchal Suchet, as well as founders of congregations, Father Colin and Father Champagnat, and future missionaries and priests of the diocese. When Lyon was spared two cholera epidemics, Victor Orsel was commissioned to do a large votive painting. His immense allegorical work,

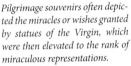

unfinished at his death in 1852, was meant to hang in the vast church designed by A. M. Chenavard, Bossan's professor of architecture. A dome would have topped the edifice, accessible via a monumental stairway from Lyon – but where would it be built?

Pilgrimages to Mary's places of worship gave rise to many canticles which enlivened the processions.

Pilgrimage souvenirs often depicted the miracles or wishes granted by statues of the Virgin, which were then elevated to the rank of miraculous representations.

The condition of the observatory and the presence of the golden Virgin allow us to date this photo of Fourvière hill between 1852 and 1859.

This photo of the torn up grounds shows the first work just before the start of construction on the new church.

The Virgin, from Black to Gold

In the early 19th century, there was plenty of available land on the hill. Pious men including Claudine Thévenet and Antoine Chevrier, founded their works and congregations here. The ex-voto by Pierre Guérin (1822) shows a "Providence" (orphanage), adjacent to the chapel. Pauline Jaricot took up the task of buying back properties which had been privatised in 1793, in order to restore them as places of faith. In 1832, she bought the Bréda property, where Chenavard built a chapel dedicated to Saint Philomène, so dear to the Curé d'Ars. Her brother, Philéas, provided a home for the women's order Jésus-Marie, while Pauline gave the Jesuits the land next to the chapel (now the museum). After the Canut silk workers' revolt, it was feared that the chapel would disappear behind fortifications, because "If Fourvière is destroyed, Lyon will be lost." An observatory was built (Pollet, 1830), bringing to the hill both science, in the form of a telescope, and commerce, in the form of a bistro. Daguerreotypes (Dolard, 1843), panoramic photos, paintings and lithographs of the era give us an idea of these random constructions. Several scenes were published in the "Album du Lyonnais" (Dauzats, 1846; Appian, 1852). Fourvière's fame reached even the far-flung Catholic missions, as can be seen in an 1847 ex-voto sent from New Caledonia.

By 1849, the old bell tower was on the verge of collapsing. Emotions ran high and the chapter of Saint-Jean wanted to demolish everything. The Rector of Fourvière (Puillet) asked a young architect, Alphonse Duboys, to draw up plans for a new church. Paul Brac de la

Above : in Lyon, in the old chapel, the Immaculate Conception was venerated many centuries before the proclamation of the dogma (mosaic of the Immaculate Conception).

Opposite, right : the Virgin of Lourdes was also made by Fabisch (mosaic of the Immaculate Conception).

Opposite, left : the house of Pauline Jaricot, at the bottom of the Rosaire garden, is built on walls from the medieval period.

Souvenir of the 1852 inauguration, with processions, miracles,
and the Virgin turned towards
the spectator and not towards
Lyon.

p.17: a close-up of the famous
5.6-metre statue reveals unexpected subtleties.

On 8 December, powerful pro-
jectors illuminate the building,
creating surprising effects.
(Year 2000)

Perrière took it upon himself to "save
(Lyon) from such deplorable experi-
ments." In the royalist "Gazette de Lyon"
(6 January 1850), Blanchon mentions a
"large beautiful church (at Fourvière)
which future generations will complete,
alongside the present church" – an al-
lusion to the project by Pierre Bossan,
which Brac de la Perrière reviewed in
July 1850.

Within the recently re-established brotherhood, the idea emerged for a "colossal golden Virgin which travellers
could venerate from a distance." The idea of a statue as a kind of signal,
later used by Marseille and its mystic beacon (1866), was expected to
bring fame to the Fourvière pilgrimage, now rivalled by La Salette's ap-
parition of the Virgin in September 1846. On Fourvière hill, the lack of
land around the chapel meant that the solution would have to be vertical. The owner of the observatory refused the use of his property and
so the Virgin would have to be mounted on the bell tower by Duboys.

On 13 December, a permit was granted to erect "a colossal statue of Notre-Dame made of golden metal as a symbol of gratitude." A competition was launched for the design of a statue measuring 5.6 metres, on a 3-metre base. Bonnassieux, winner of the Prix de Rome, lost out to Joseph-Hugues Fabisch, a professor at the Lyon School of Fine Arts. His design was cast by Lanfrey and Baud, after numerous changes to the plaster moulds. The statue was seen as a great technical feat, which earned Fabisch a commission for the statue of Lourdes. Bonnassieux got his revenge in 1860 with his design for the 16-metre high Virgin of Le Puy, known as the Black Virgin.

The golden Virgin, unveiled in great pomp by Cardinal Bonald, was an immediate success. Two years before the proclamation in Rome of the dogma of the Immaculate Conception, the faithful of Lyon could look up daily in veneration of their Virgin. On the evening of 8 December 1852, the cardinal wept with joy when he saw the entire city illuminated "from the humblest abode to the noblest chateau." This was the first time a celebration of Mary was so widely followed, though some used the strong winds that evening as an excuse not to participate. The decorations, lanterns (known as chelus) and candle lamps scintillated in the night, coinciding with the visit of Sheik Abdel Kader. The affection of the locals for Mary of the humble people embarrassed the "Lords of Fourvière," still hoping for a grandiose new church, but who opted for a more discrete takeover of the hill which would then allow them to move forward with their project.

Fronton of the Saint Thomas of Canterbury chapel. This place of worship was designed by Sainte-Marie Perrin to replace the nave which had been destroyed to build a sacristy.

Bottom: on 8 December, many people prefer the traditional candle lamps to the megawatt displays around town.

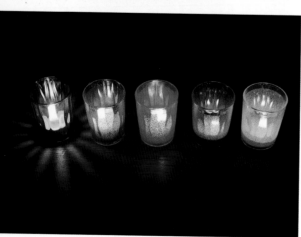

"When the time comes"

Son of a Lyon merchant, Pierre Bossan left the studio of Labrouste in Paris to return to Lyon when his father died, around 1839. His taste for Gothic design won him the position as chief architect of Saint Jean Cathedral. On Quai Fulchiron, between the recently restored Saint Georges Church, and the commandery of Saint Georges de Jérusalem (later destroyed by fire), he built a "Moorish" edifice where, it is said, he forgot to provide for the stairs. The rich Catholic owner, Joannès Blanchon, became a dedicated admirer. Something of a Catholic citadel, located between two church monuments, the seemingly fortified building, boasts a large statue of Mary. Today, we can still admire this first, and unfortunately last, example of the exceptional collaboration between Bossan and Blanchon.

In 1846, Bossan launched himself into an ill-advised industrial venture. His brother, an engineer at the Ecole des Mines of Alès, won him a contract to build a gas plant. According to his lawyer, Brac de la Perrière, the bankruptcy of the gas company put Bossan in deep trouble: his family was evicted, his sisters forced to work, his assets seized. Bossan fled to Palermo. His brother joined him there but soon died in an epidemic. Bossan, of Mediterranean origin, was impressed by the cathedral and the Arab palaces of Monreale. While in Palermo, he may have started working on plans for a new church at Fourvière, which he completed upon his return to Lyon. In Rome, between late 1849 and mid 1850, he worked with the architects Louis Perret and Frédéric Giniez, illustrating their great book on the catacombs.

Sketch of Bossan during his visit to the Curé d'Ars, by Borel, for the decoration of the church in Ars.

To the right of the Vow of Louis XIII appears a group of famous Catholics, Chateaubriand next to Bonaparte, Jacquard and Hippolyte Flandrin.

His plans for Fourvière, lost on the return trip from Italy when the boat nearly sank, but later found under a barrel, began to attract attention but were rejected in June 1850 by Cardinal de Bonald. Already committed to building a large number of parish churches, the cardinal criticized the cost of Bossan's project and the narrowness of the lateral naves. Brac de la Perrière retorted that, "His Holiness thinks he is a good judge of architecture, but in fact he knows nothing about it." A prolific drawer, Bossan provided his sister Françoise's workshop with models for embroidery motifs and banners, in part to pay off a debt of over 52,600 francs, but also out of sheer drive. The Bossan sisters' vestment shop, the architect's office and the studio of painter Louis Janmot were all at the same location, at 51 Cours Rambaud. Janmot was completing "Poème de l'Âme" (now at the Lyon Fine Arts Museum), and the two men developed a deep mutual appreciation during that time.

Janmot's mystic symbolism and his taste for writing find their equivalent in the basilica, in the form of angels, the strong use of texts and especially the vertical ascension of the design. Certain Lyon artists tended to group with like-minded writers, such as Ballanche and Blanc de Saint-Bonnet, all of them more or less influenced by Illuminism (Lyon had been the European capital of this form of religious mysticism in the 18th century). Neo-Platonism and Idealism, as taught by Abbot Noirot, influenced such leading figures as Frédéric Ozanam and Hippolyte Flandrin, whose portraits appear in "The Vow of Louis XIII."

According to Bossan, after his turbulent youth, he was converted by the Curé d'Ars in about 1852, thanks to his sisters. As he put it, "Italy gave me direction, Ars gave me independence." Bossan also owed a great deal to his father, a well-known businessman, and Labrouste, who taught him certain elements of decoration. "When the time comes, you will find everything you need," predicted the Curé d'Ars, in 1858. That long-awaited "time" was the prime concern of the Fourvière Commission, founded in March 1853 by Cardinal de Bonald and which included influential laity. Bossan became involved in the Fourvière project after the sudden death of Duboys, in May 1853. The first President of the Commission, Antoine Frapet, was the father-in-law of Johannès Blanchon. Already Prefect of the secret congregation of Jesuits, Blanchon became the Secretary of the Commission, and its driving force. It took 17 years of hard work and the threat of a Prussian invasion for the "time" to finally arrive.

Left: the sainted teacher, Jean-Baptiste de la Salle stands with Benoît Labre and the Curé d'Ars, in this stained glass window known as "Mary queen of the Confessors."

Right: consecration of the parish of Ars, dated some 20 years before the proclamation of the dogma of the Immaculate Conception.

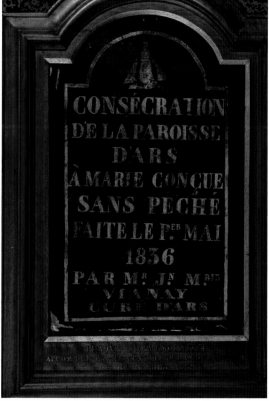

Fourvière: the dream

Many historic varieties of roses can be found in the Rosaire garden.

The engraving by Séon was the first representation of Fourvière church, made public during the sensational World Fair of 1855.

Building the new church would require purchasing a good portion of the hill. A lottery and donations made it possible to acquire the observatory and to gain the Commission's full independence from the chapter of Saint Jean Cathedral. The observatory was reduced by one storey in 1858. The land belonging to Miss Jaricot and Miss Rocoffort, at the foot of the chapel, was targeted next. Pauline Jaricot had lost all her money in mystical-industrial enterprises which may have ensured her place in heaven, but in the meantime made her life hell in Fourvière. Various tricks deprived her of a modest income from a toll path (1853-1856) which could have paid off her smallest creditors. In her tracts, she wrote of "hindrances" and "spoliation." Upon her death, the Commission acquired her house, known as Lorette. On these slopes, Bossan and Fabisch set up 15 commemorative markers as a symbol of

F-BOSSAN INV.

AVANT - PROJET DE

N · D · DE FOURVIÈRE

APPROUVÉ PAR SON EM-

LE CARDINAL DE BONALD

the mysteries of the Rosary (1864), also evoked in the white roses of the mosaic of the Immaculate Conception. Today's rose garden symbolizes the virtues of the Virgin and at the same time pays homage to the creations of Lyon's great rose cultivators.

Bossan's original drawings for Fourvière were lost after their publication in 1891. According to Quincieu, they were "sketched and re-worked without erasing previous lines." Bossan drew more as a visionary than as an architect and his drawings have a frail poetry to them. The sharp point of a pale lead pencil chooses from the infinite possibilities of a first interlacing of lines, to extract the ideal form, in much the same way the silhouette of the basilica gradually emerges from the morning fog.

Bossan drew a gigantic central keep to raise the statue of the Virgin. He was trying to soften the widespread disappointment when the statue of Saint Michael appeared on top of the church, instead of Fabisch's golden Virgin.

Fourvière as it was meant to be seen. This utopian vision of a green hillside is an attack against Pauline Jaricot's toll road to the church via a rather unattractive stairway.

FOURVIÈRE TEL QU'IL DEVRAIT-ÊTRE.

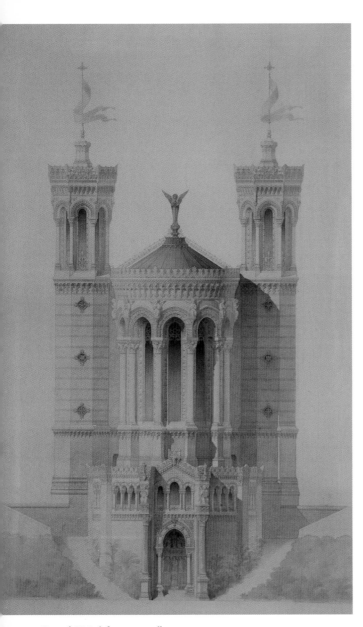

One of Giniez' finest aquarelles shows the finest part of Fourvière, the apse.

The final draft of the project was entrusted to the engraver Séon, just as the sensational World Fair of 1855 was closing in Paris. In Lyon, Séon's engraving elicited some amusement; according to Paul de Saint-Olive, "it is quite simply a fantasy." Séon's work presented the church on a very difficult location on the edge of the plateau, giving an impressive, towering effect; the unified volume of the nave encases the main supporting structures, and the circular choir tops the nave like a dot on an i. Added to this is an unlikely conjoining of the old church with the new; the old bell tower with its golden Virgin appears in the engraving as if it was a tower of the new church. A message of encouragement from Pius IX inspired Bossan to complete his project while in Rome in 1858.

Bossan's large drawings (41.8 x 29 cm) were entrusted to the talented aquarellist Frédéric Giniez, in 1863. In his studio on Quai Tilsitt, with its view of Fourvière, Giniez painted large aquarelles of incomparable virtuosity. Superb photos, no doubt by Fatalot, drew attention to the project. The aquarelles showed several variations, such as the vaulted ceilings which were no longer quite so Gothic. Giniez' works marked the first serious recognition of the new Fourvière church. Presented at the great exhibition of religious art at Rome in 1869, they earned Bossan a prestigious pontifical award.

Around 1870, the project was given new hope thanks to the disappearance of its main obstacles: Cardinal de Bonald and the occupant of the needed land, then the hostile rector, followed by the influential architect, C. A. Benoît, who withdrew his own project. The Fourvière Commission, the driving force behind the project, proclaimed its "providential mission" on 8 October 1870. In an aquarelle by Lameire, we see angels carrying the model of Fourvière up to heaven.

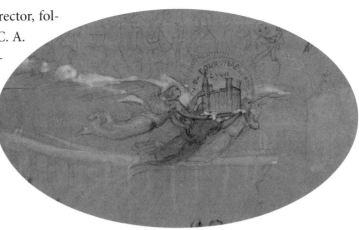

The architects at work

Just as Christ is the invisible head of the Catholic Church, Bossan became the invisible head of Fourvière Church. Almost as soon as work began, he moved away to La Ciotat, near Toulon. This caused a degree of consternation and there were speculations as to the reasons: his mother's origins in the Marseille region, or his health, but officially, he was "down on his knees drawing the plans." The artist seemed somehow to be fleeing the realisation of an old dream, or legal troubles in Échallon and a bothersome family in Lyon. Bossan also gave up his school of sacred art in Valence, to devote himself to building a Dominican convent in Marseille, ordered in 1869, and to manage a marble business in Cereyste. At his extremely uncomfortable studio in La Ciotat, he trained Millefaut, with his usual severity, to make the models of the sculptures for Fourvière. According to Sainte-Marie Perrin, Bossan lived in complete austerity, which is confirmed by the inventory of his estate upon his death. Though legend has it that he ate slugs, he apparently washed them down with fine wine, listed in the inventory, no doubt Noilly-Prat made by the patroness of the Marseille convent! His library revealed the influence of Maria d'Agreda. He had an impressive annual salary of 13,000 gold francs (1880): in just one week, he earned the equivalent of 1000 hours of a labourer, which was not unusual, but certainly confirms his fame.

"La Semaine Illustrée" published a feature on the laying of the first stone, on 7 December 1872. The ceremony was held in the excavation pit for the apse, 26 metres deep, with a crowd of clergy and curious onlookers.

The variety of stones used at Fourvière is one of the best ideas of Sainte-Marie Perrin. He took advantage of the know-how of Charles Garnier's work at the Opera House of Paris and went personally to many quarries.

As of 1871, Sainte-Marie Perrin (1835-1917) was already acting as the visible head architect of Fourvière, to the great disappointment of Bossan's other colleagues. The Perrin brothers were well ensconced among the Catholic community of Lyon. Louis, known as Sainte-Marie, was the son-in-law of the architect Desjardins, a friend of Bossan. His sisters were in the same convent as Thérèse Bossan. His brother, a lawyer, worked for Brac de la Perrière and was, like Sainte-Marie, a member of the discrete congregation of laity, founded by the Jesuits. After training under the architect Questel and the decorator Dénuelle, in Paris, Sainte-Marie Perrin quickly made a name for himself as an architect and talented designer. Like Blanchon, he was cowed by the imposing figure of Bossan, his prophet-like demeanour, his extreme reserve, his visual and mental sharpness. But his enemies called him the "old fox" and in 1890 Janmot complained of his tyranny and habit of "consulting only himself" in matters of decoration, dictating orders to the artists, who were relegated to the role of mere "extras."

But over their 16 years of collaboration, Sainte-Marie Perrin came to consider Bossan as something of a spiritual leader. The project became a work of faith, "like a castle built for God," wrote Perrin's son-in-law, Paul Claudel, "This church which you have built for Mary, through much suffering, naïve yet knowing, like your soul, and clear, like your conscience."

Correspondence between the two architects gives us exceptional insight into the life of the project. Twice a year, Sainte-Marie went to La Ciotat, whose train station appeared in one of the first films of the Lumière brothers, made shortly before the inauguration of Fourvière. Bossan, from afar, demanded corrections; he visited Fourvière perhaps a dozen times. His visit in 1874 was particularly agitated: "I can't get over it," he wrote to Sainte-Marie Perrin. He advised Perrin to be extremely prudent in his dealings with the Commission and he resorted to a passive yet efficient resistance which enabled him to keep the crypt and his price quote of 791,103 francs. Though Bossan was mostly absent, Blanchon was so present on the worksite that he was often referred to as the third architect. He went all over the city to view the effect from afar. He made several key contributions, including his ingenious idea to use the soil removed during the excavations, to fill in the gap to the north of the building and create a large esplanade. Despite it's ample dimensions, the esplanade proved barely sufficient to accommodate the crowds for the Eucharistic Congress in 1939, and today can barely handle the tourist coaches which come from all over Europe. Nearby, Bossan built an interesting neo-rural house for the chaplains. Following the death of Bossan's faithful contractor, Sainte-Marie Perrin switched to a direct management system, which he claimed to be more "moral" because

Assembly of bishops in the mosaic of the Immaculate Conception. Lameire amused himself by representing his friend Sainte-Marie Perrin as an Oriental prelate; his adolescent son Antoine, is in the foreground, leaning against the balustrade.

The plaster modellos were made in Bossan's studio in La Ciotat, mostly by Millefaut, then shipped to Fourvière.

Modello for the fronton: portrait of the presidents of the Fourvière Commission: P. Dugas, who died in 1875, and A. de Boissieu, who died in 1886.

each craftsman would be in charge of his own work, but the neo-medieval Jésus-Ouvrier corporation of sculptors (1889), was a failure.

Correspondence between the architects gives evidence of occasional surprises on the worksite, which might be put down to "pious imprudence." One subject of concern was the fact that the models of the sculptures, now at Fourvière museum, proved to be more life-like than their enlarged sculpted stone versions.

ANGE AGENOUILLÉ
Réalisé en trois exemplaires, se situant sous le porche de
la façade principale.
THE KNEELING ANGEL
Three examples, situated beneath the porch of the front facade.
Date imprécise – Milieu... – Date unknown
« IN N PATRIS ET FILII ET SPIRITU.S »

Opposite: stored in the attic after a fire in the worksite sheds, the modellos are being gradually restored and displayed at the museum. They seem to better express the talent of the sculptors than the full-size renditions in stone for the basilica.

Below, left: the griffon, a mythical being with the body of a lion and the head and wings of an eagle, fighting in the army of the Good.

Below, right: the church is populated with numerous angels, all soldiers in the army of the Good. Alongside Archangel Michael, they fight the Evil enemy of heaven and earth, their sins and heresies, commanded by Satan and his acolytes.

TÊTE D'ANGE
Placée au-dessus de chaque chapelle.
ANGEL'S HEAD

29

From the beginning

After a full year of review, Bossan's project was accepted, on condition that the price be lowered substantially. He therefore reduced the dimensions by 1/20th and moved the church back further onto the plateau. This made it impossible to connect the two churches. After heated discussions, Bossan left Valence to manage the location aspects. A 26-metre trench was dug to build the apse. The solemn inauguration on 7 December was widely covered in the press. The quarry proved insufficient to meet the demand for high-quality Tarascon limestone. Sainte-Marie Perrin drew up the bonding design, the cutting lines, joints and surface (roughening). An enormous cylindrical base was built to hold the circular choirs of the upper and lower naves. This

Of the many photos taken of the worksite, only a few remain. The building is about to receive the roof (circa 1879), the metal framework is ready for the slate tiles. We see the scaffolding in the back and the incomplete Tower of Justice.

strange dungeon is surrounded by a seven-sided rectilinear wall which houses the double stairway to the crypt. The vaulted ceiling is a masterpiece of stone-cutting and bonding, while the openings onto the garden are framed by charmingly Byzantine columns.

The upper level has two galleries. The lower one has rows of arches and is covered, while the upper one is uncovered and connects to the upper nave. From this vantage point, the Prelate blesses the city with the ostensorium, in accordance with 17th century ritual, now permanently set in the church's architecture. Arched mouldings made of marble from Baveno (Lago Maggiore, Italy) top the door known as the Porte des Lions, in tribute to the archaeologist Schlieman, famous for the digs at Mycenae. Less ornately carved than originally planned, the apse nonetheless gives a hint of the magnificence to come. Blanchon conducted tours of it every Sunday. The worshiper would enter the

The door of the Lions (left): construction began with this door. A comparison with the draft project (right) shows that this prestigious section was never completed. It was meant to be the main entrance for pilgrims, moving from Joseph to Mary.

31

building by the Porte des Lions, after a pious ascension of the hill via the Rosary Garden. The Porte des Lions is one of the strange errors of Fourvière. In 1884, citing reasons of safety, Cardinal Caverot imposed a Western access to the crypt, which eliminated the usefulness of the superb apse, ignored thereafter, and the Porte des Lions was never given its lions.

The crypt is dedicated to Saint Joseph, linking the Old and New Testaments, and worshipers are meant to go "to Mary via Joseph." The lower church evokes the darkness of humanity which has not yet received the Light. It is called a crypt, out of habit, but it is in fact a lower church whose northern bays give sparse light to the vaulted ceiling, barely 10 metres high. The pillars are shortened by capitals which are topped by stone courses in a Byzantine style. The overall impression is rather oppressing. There are a multitude of architectural oddities, arches doubled for no reason, choir columns set back in the wall as if by force, upside-down groins, with their points at the bottom, side niches and a nearly circular choir. In 1878, Ernest Renan visited the site unannounced and saw the still undecorated nave; he stated that, "Since antiquity, I have never seen respect for the divine taken quite so far."

Intent on giving a sample of the future splendour of the monument, Bossan, offered his wages for the year 1880 (13,000 francs) in order to decorate the choir. His portrait, as a dying Saint Joseph, on the altar tomb, was an act of devotion as well as a remembrance of his young brother Joseph, who died in Palermo. As in Lalouvesc, another church

Many worshipers of Portuguese origin are happy to find an image of the Virgin of Fatima.

Death of Joseph : at the altar tomb in the crypt, Millefaut sculpted the death of Saint Joseph, with Bossan's features. The architect venerated the Virgin's husband. This was the first decoration of the church, offered by Bossan.

designed by Bossan, sumptuous mosaics were chosen to decorate the vaulted ceilings, beautifully highlighting the white marble angels personifying the Beatitudes. A year before Bossan's death, the gigantic statue of Saint Joseph holding a child was completed, giving bold definition to the iconographic meaning of the entire monument.

The crypt choir is entirely decorated with mosaics, on the theme of the evangelical Beatitudes which Saint Joseph so perfectly embodied. Eight sculpted angels carry the symbols of the eight non-violent traits (left to right: 1 – crown, poor; 2 – lamb, gentle; 3 – tears, bereaved; 4 – scales, just; 5 – sheathed sword, merciful; 6 – lily, pure; 7 – dove, peacemaker; 8 – chains, persecuted). The mosaic of the jack arch shows the evangelical texts and angels. The architecture of the nave is somewhat oppressive yet expressive and almost expressionist.

Emerging into the light

Going up the steps in front of the great western façade, visitors encounter the Lion of Judah, Joseph's tribe. The lion stands guard in front of the stairway to the crypt. Sculpted by Dufraine, in granite, for eternity, the lion seems to emerge from ancient times to welcome the new era. The main façade (west) is itself a monument within the monument. Its depth is accentuated from the first step of the flight of stairs all the way to the great revolving doors of oak, built under the tribune in order to break the typically strong winds of the site. The towers give balance to the composition, both physically, by their sheer mass, and visually, by the power they convey. The visitor then passes the columns of the porch. Twenty-two horses were needed to carry the 15 tonnes of red granite from La Balma (Lago Maggiore, Italy) for these columns. Legend has it that crowds of people covered the convoy with flowers.

Above the porch, the gallery of angels, leaning over the entrance, gives lightness to the upper wall. Nine caryatid angels seem to effortlessly carry the colossal weight of the fronton. Millefaut took care not to overly carve the Echaillon limestone in order to maintain the strength of these supporting elements. The gallery of angels hides a wall whose massive bonding (a single layer of enormous rectangular blocks) is visible from the tribune, and which offers a magical view over the nave.

The large triangle of the fronton caps the linear composition of the façade. The upper edges reach towards the summit of the towers. The geometry of the composition has visibly been calculated according to the "divine proportion", or Phi. The sculpted scene represents the prayers answered by the Virgin. In this portrait gallery, we see, on the right, the bishops who supported the project, kneeling next to the Virgin and surrounded by the Archangels Michael and Raphael, in a reminder of the vow of 1870. On the left are the successive presidents of the Fourvière Commission, dressed as the town councillors who made the first vow in 1643. The poor souls suffering from the plague are in fact Bossan, on the right, and Blanchon, on the left, as a reminder of the great epidemic which Lyon escaped, thanks to Mary's intervention. Most of the people depicted in this scene were dead by the time of the inauguration, except Cardinal Coullié, presenting the model, and Blanchon, who had gone blind.

Top: the door of the Lions has no lions, but we can see in the unsculpted stone where they would have been, and their lying position, which is typical of the style in southern France, e.g. the cathedral of Embrun.

Bottom: the lion is the symbol of the tribe of Judah – Joseph's tribe. This is why a granite lion is guarding the entry to the crypt.

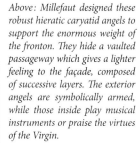

Above: Millefaut designed these robust hieratic caryatid angels to support the enormous weight of the fronton. They hide a vaulted passageway which gives a lighter feeling to the façade, composed of successive layers. The exterior angels are symbolically armed, while those inside play musical instruments or praise the virtues of the Virgin.

The winged emblems of the evangelists (known as the Tetramorph), under the gallery of angels: the eagle of Saint John, the lion of Saint Mark, the man of Saint Luke, the bull of Saint Mathew.

p.39, top: view of the upper elements: the juxtaposition of the
two churches shows the clear do-
mination of the colossal dimensions of the basilica.

p. 39, bottom: the metal ties and
the inversed volume of the three
domes gives the attic a technical
look, far removed from the unity
and grandeur of the nave.

A drawing from the worksite
shows one of the towers with its
decorations which were never
carried out.

The day of the inauguration, the enormous bronze doors, cast in Paris, opened up to reveal the symbols of the alliances sealed between
God and Man, as represented by the Arch of Alliance and Noah's Ark.
Those who come to worship are seized by the breathtaking entrance to
the nave in the upper church. They are subjugated, pulled in from all
sides, manipulated as in a baroque design, then swept up to the heights
of the building. They are humbled by the massive stylobates (column
supports). The thin columns of "blue" marble from Séez, (near Bourg-
Saint-Maurice, in the Tarentaise region of Savoy), seem to be suspen-
ded from the shimmering vaulted ceiling, covered with mosaic images
of Mary. The unified and imposing volume balances the thrust of the
walls and vaults. In front of the exterior pillars, the vaults are topped
with false tribunes, encasing the side altars at their base. A small sketch
by Sainte-Marie Perrin shows the stone lintel which braces this cle-
ver balance. Another sketch shows the general balance of the building,
from the ground up, and shows the wagons of materials placed at the
top of the walls to build the three domes. By climbing up the observatory tower, a unique world is revealed.

Flying with the angels

At the summit of the "windy tower" (the public observatory), two colossal forces meet: that of a horizon reaching all the way to the Alps,
and that of Mary's fortress. The silhouettes of the four towers are the
identifying feature of the monument seen from every direction. They
represent the four cardinal virtues of Mary: Prudence and Temperance
(facing the city of merchants), and Strength and Justice (on each side
of the façade). The crenels, of Hispano-Moorish inspiration, were never carved. The connection of the towers to the side walls was a great
challenge, as was the correspondence between the cylindrical interior
and the octagonal exterior shell. The stairs of the observatory form a
superb spiral, attached to powerful corbelling with unexpected motifs.
A scientific observatory was installed when the Catholic University was
established in Lyon, bringing science and faith together in one place.

The towers are not in fact part of the main structure and are more symbolic than useful: too narrow to be used as a sacristy, and too fragile to hold the larger bells, which had been cast, mounted, then taken down at great cost. The additional tower, which was meant to raise Mary higher than Michael, is one of the myths associated with Fourvière. Anonymous letters denounced a swindle; the campanile, bell tower, light tower and pedestals all remained on the drawing board. The banners designed by Giniez were flown for the inauguration in 1896, but could not be raised in 1986 for the visit of Pope John-Paul II, because the necessary know-how had been lost.

Though the towers are the most ostentatious feature of Fourvière, the roof of the building is a technical marvel. A passageway, made of limestone from Villebois, goes fully round the building, running behind the fronton, which is higher than the roof, due to an indispensable optical correction made necessary by the distance from the ground. On the back side of the fronton, a commemorative plaque marks the laying of the final stone, in 1884. Vertical lead pipes, rising from the passageway, evacuate the rain water from the roof to an underground reservoir, used for sprinkling.

Spiral staircase: the stairway of the Tower of Justice, encased in the cylindrical walls of the tower, almost looks like a snail shell when viewed from the bottom.

The roof frame, originally designed to be made of oak, was replaced in 1874 with an innovative metal system, already used at La Salette, which bears the extreme load (27 kg/sq. m.) of the slate tiles from Angers, specially cut in large plates, and attached with hooks. A conical covering, independent of the main roof, tops the circular choir. Under the two-sided roof, the vast space of the nave appears, punctuated by the mounds of the three domes. The vertiginous plunge to the ground can be seen via a few holes cut into the thickness of the vaulted ceiling, giving a true appreciation of the spectacular dimensions of the building.

A golden house for Mary

Bossan dreamed of a church that would be a Golden House, finely chisel-led like the work of a goldsmith. In 1857, he made designs for Favier, a goldsmith of religious art objects, but he developed closer working relations with Armand-Calliat (1860). This self-taught goldsmith was, like Bossan, fascinated by all things mystical and how to express them with gold and precious stones. They both believed in the Biblical conception of wealth, proclaiming with the psalms, *Domine dilexi decorem domus tuae* (Lord, I love the splendour of your house). Starting in 1867, and with the help of Canon Didelot de Valence, an excellent Bible scholar, the two artists created many remarkable iconographies. The mystical inspiration is particularly spectacular in the monumental ostensoriums which give a hint of the iconography to come at Fourvière. The ostensorium of Fourvière (1878) is a work of poetry, telling of God's revelation to Man. We are lifted in ascension, from the shepherds and the wise men at the bottom, to Joseph and Mary. The revelation culminates with the physical presence of God, in the consecrated bread, in the centre of a burst of light. As on the shaft of an ostensorium, the iconography of Fourvière church unfolds vertically along the mystical axis formed by Saint Michael's lance.

Gold appears in careful touches in the decoration of the church, mostly in the mosaics, used throughout the building, to the great disappointment of painters such as Janmot. The fine golden tessera of Venice were used to great effect in La-louvesc, then in the crypt of Fourvière. A golden background is used in smaller areas, while the blue representing Mary is used on the larger surfaces of the vaulted ceilings. In the wall mosaics by Lameire, gold is used to highlight, never to dominate. Some sculptures have gold touches; the little angels are golden. The nave is "bursting with enamels and marble, bronze and gold," wrote Huysmans in 1890. The tempered shine of the large bronzes, the ciborium, and the trimming of the altars sets off the sacred golden objects.

Above: the unity of the nave is inspired by the Romanesque art of southern France, which reduces the side areas to mere aisles. A balance is achieved in the nave thanks to the upper tribunes which neutralise the arch thrust and rest on surprisingly thin columns.
p.43: a view from the upper levels is necessary to grasp the dynamics of the space, dilated as in baroque art.
Below: this mosaic in the choir is one of the more heavily gilded of the church, with a very Byzantine splendour.

The liturgical vestments sparkle with the movement of the clergy, in a well-practiced ballet. The circular layout of the choir adds to the impression of distancing the faithful from the officiating priest, in the Byzantine style. The grandiose liturgy, the organ, the choirs, the smoke of the incense and even the fashions of the ladies in the pews contribute to this mystical ambiance. According to Blanchon, the richness appealed to the public as something of "a fulfilment of their own desires." Only the large white statues are spared from all the extravagance. They take their strength from a sort of absence, but an active one, in the Asian sense, which asserts the power of innocence, the only force capable of defying evil. This wondrous composition culminates with the statue of Mary, at the main altar. The luxury of the decor showcases her great virtue, which needs no adornment.

The winged creatures give a feeling of other-worldliness, accentuated by their position in the upper reaches of the building.

Above: a little castle seems to be hidden in the church. In fact it is the bastion taking up the arch thrust. It connects to the great space of the monument via columns which frame it an unexpected manner.

Opposite: the vaulting of the three domes is Bossan's way of definitively abandoning the gothic style of his youth, and at the same time giving ample space for this exceptional image of Mary.

p.47: Saint Michael brandishing
his lance symbolises the fight
of Good against Evil, which
is repeated throughout the
building.

The great battle between Good and Evil

Below: the monumental keystone of the choir, six metres in diameter, is cut like a jewel, reflecting the Holy Ghost. It is also one of the focal points of the symbolic axis running from the lance of Saint Michael on the roof, down through the church.

Jesus' name appears over the door of the tabernacle of the crypt's altar. The tessera of the mosaic are set in the white marble with absolute technical perfection.

The arrival of the monumental statue of Saint Michael set off a furore. Cast in the same workshop as the Statue of Liberty made for New York, the statue of Saint Michael was erected in 1882 at the top of the conical roof over the apse, where the golden statue of the Virgin was meant to be. Bossan imposed this costly figure, despite heated opposition from all sides, including on the part of Blanchon. Some saw in the Archangel the symbol of the Count of Chambord and it is true that Bossan, as he himself admitted, was hoping for a "visit of Henri V to Fourvière and a donation from Saint Michael." The unexpected death of the Pretender to the throne left little hope of finding a benefactor and a rather large bill to be paid. The Illuminists, along with certain Freemasons, believed in the idea of a huge final battle between Good and Evil; the supreme leader of the Good is the Archangel Michael, whom Bossan considered as a "figure of the Virgin."

Michael's star-studded lance, thrust vertically towards the mouth of the dragon, defines the axis of a gigantomachy piercing through the strata of the entire church, from top to bottom. The Archangel commands the troops of Good, the guardian angels, the caryatides of the façade, the Beatitudes, the Magnificat and litanies. Saint Michael is the leader of the valorous lions - of Judah and Lyon. The Archangel presides over all battles: be it David against Goliath, Judith against Holophern, or Jacob against the angel. The enormous dove of the Holy Ghost, on the keystone of the choir, commands all the birds of Good, the eagles and peacocks, and all of the virtues, be they cardinal (the towers), theological (north external bays) or those attributed to the gentle sex: chastity and humi-

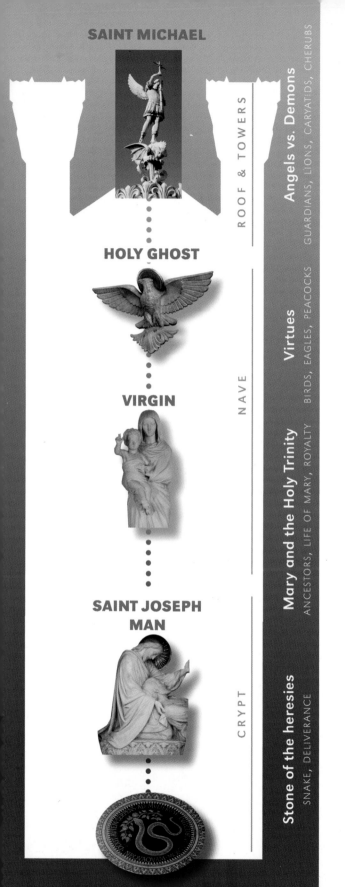

SAINT MICHAEL

ROOF & TOWERS

Angels vs. Demons

GUARDIANS, LIONS, CARYATIDS, CHERUBS

HOLY GHOST

NAVE

Virtues

BIRDS, EAGLES, PEACOCKS

VIRGIN

Mary and the Holy Trinity

ANCESTORS, LIFE OF MARY, ROYALTY

SAINT JOSEPH
MAN

CRYPT

Stone of the heresies

SNAKE, DELIVERANCE

lity (south exterior wall). Starting from the Holy Ghost, and continuing across the three cupolas to the fronton of the great west door is a horizontal branch of Mary's family tree, inspired by Maria d'Agreda's vision of Mary according to God. Stained glass works around the nave depict the royalty of Mary, the verses of the Magnificat and the litanies of the Virgin.

After crossing through the "stone of the heresies" (from Arianism to Lutheranism), the axis reaches the ambassador of Good, Saint Joseph with child, surrounded by the Beatitudes and Eucharistic emblems in the stained glass windows. But Evil, symbolized by the "stone of sin", acts as the base of the entire edifice. Instead of showing the effects of sin in Man – what could be easier than to paint a criminal, weapon in hand? – Sainte-Marie Perrin, on the advice of Émile Mâle, used animals to depict human vice. We therefore see a "greedy" ant and a "slothful" turtle! Bossan was a fervent but discrete disciple of Maria d'Agreda. This visionary Spanish Franciscan (1602- 1665) gave virginal interpretations of sacred texts, which she drew from her visions. Bossan had a copy of the 18th century translation by Père Crozet of "Mystical City of God", in which the nun describes a mystical castle, with four towers in the name of the theological virtues – a clear inspiration for Fourvière church. The

Opposite: the symbolic axis pierces the building from top to bottom, running through layers of good and evil.
p.49: the immaculate whiteness of the statue of Mary imposes itself amidst the ostentation of the gilt elements. It is the embodiment of the strength of innocence.

nun suggested a virginal perspective on Biblical texts, in particular the Canticle of Canticles. Several themes found at Fourvière can be directly attributed to the writings of Maria d'Agreda. From the binary formula, indicating the divine origins of the Virgin, "the Word will have on earth a mother without father, as it has in heaven a father without mother," Bossan took the ternary theme of the three cupolas of the upper nave: "Mary, Daughter of God the Father, Spouse of God the Holy Ghost, Mother of God the Son." Maria d'Agreda also used texts known to all Catholics: the Magnificat and the litanies of the Virgin.

In the book published for the inauguration of the church, "The Symbolism of Fourvière," Sainte-Marie Perrin identified the themes and inscriptions, without citing any sources other than biblical texts. Did he really not know of Maria d'Agreda? He goes no further than to highlight the traditional correspondence between the Old and New Testaments, as later developed in the exterior sculptures by Belloni: each theological virtue (faith, hope, charity) is illustrated by its best known figures in the Bible.

Sin constitutes the base of the entire building and, typically, man seeks to lay blame on innocent animals: the peacock is accused of pride, the cat of anger and the goat of lust.

The original drawing for the Virgin of the choir.

Other times, other perspectives

An aquarelle by Lameire shows the nearly final composition of the mosaic known as "The Battle of Lépante."

Between the death of Bossan in 1888 and the inauguration of the church in 1896, many other key figures also disappeared, including the first mosaic artists, Mora and Razuret. Blanchon died in 1897. Sainte-Marie Perrin completed the very elegant connection between the old and new churches. The large decorative elements were mounted; the mosaics and sculptures of the higher sections were made using the scaffolding of the construction work. Still to be completed were the decorations of the great vertical walls of the nave and the sculpting of seven side altars, subject of some dispute between Bossan and the church authorities. Dufraine was chosen to do the fronton, which he finished just in time for the inauguration, before moving onto the first chapel (Notre-Dame de Pitié, 1899) and his final work, "La Sagesse", the year of his death, in 1900.

Pope Pius V invoking the Virgin and watching his army defeat the Turks (1571); the fleet of Selim II on fire and sinking. Following this victory of the Cross over the Crescent, Pius V established the feast day of the Rosary, held every year on the anniversary of the battle (7 October).

The Council of Ephesus: designed in 1910 by Décote, the work wasn't completed until 1946. We see Saint Cyril proclaiming the divine maternity of Mary.

p.53: stained glass work by Décote (1901-1902) representing Mary, Queen of the Prophets.

Joan of Arc: rigorous and spare design by Décote.

Most of the mural decorations in Fourvière's nave date from the 20th century, including works by Parisians such as the sculptor Guillaume, ("Wedding at Cana", 1905), the stained glass artists, Lameire the famed mosaic artist and decorator of Madeleine Church in Paris, who was also a friend of Sainte-Marie Perrin. His four mosaics for Fourvière were completed the year of his death, 1910. The iconography of the great mosaics, drawn up in 1894, moved away from the mysticism of Bossan, in favour of more militant politico-religious options, Mary and the Church, Mary and France. The "Battle of Lépante" (1900), for example, was meant to remind partisans of the Republic that, long ago, the temporal power of the Pope had saved western civilisation from the Turkish invaders. The Vow of Louis XIII, (1902) was made by Christians "horrified by the impious projects of the anticlerical ministry of Waldeck-Rousseau (1899)." Joan of Arc, the symbol of patriotism, was made by Georges Décote in 1917, upon his return from the front lines of WWI. Sainte-Marie Perrin's son was not so lucky, dying shortly before his own father.

Opposite: each stained glass panel, starting with the first in 1896, shows a different image of Mary, Queen of the Prophets (top, left), the Apostles, the Patriarchs, the Martyrs and Angels.

p. 55: in this representation of Mary as Queen of the Martyrs, Décote strikes a balance between force and tranquillity in order to preserve the overall unity.

The glasswork contains numerous superb details, such as Archangel Michael and Joan of Arc; Raphael and Tobias, Gabriel, in the 1904 work "Mary Queen of Angels"; Saint Rémy baptising Clovis, in the 1900 work "Mary Queen of the Apostles"; Saint Blandine surrounded by fierce animals in "Mary Queen of the Martyrs"; opposite, Daniel in the lion pit, in "Mary Queen of the Prophets".

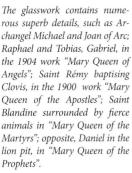

Lameire had recommended Georges Décote to Sainte-Marie Perrin for the stained glass works. A Lyon-born student of Gustave Moreau, Décote was a member of the Biblical group of Abbot Ferret, and a friend of Huysmans (1896-1898). The designs for the windows, made in about 1900, have a great unity which can be seen in the juxtaposition of the first work ("Queen of the Martyrs", 1899) and the last ("Queen of the Patriarchs", 1921). A talented decorator, colourist and designer of wall paper motifs, Décote preserved the overall harmony of the setting. He tempered the brightness of the glass, on the advice of Sainte-Marie Perrin, and developed variations on the theme of Mary's royalty.

Reminiscent of the Viennese hieratic style, the stained glass windows were spared the criticism aimed at Fourvière's excessive luxury. In 1864, when architect Paul Abadie, author of the drawings for Montmartre, saw Giniez' aquarelles of Fourvière, he was at first charmed by them, but later rejected what he called its "Bataclan" look, a slang term meaning useless decoration, and which later became the name of a famous cabaret. Abadie's criticism can be seen as a precursor of the fashion for extreme sobriety, at its height in 1945. Fourvière's extravagance was despised, resulting in little effort to maintain the edifice and the loss of certain archives.

The bare stones of the west tower were entrusted to Larrivé (1917-1920). They imposed certain constraints on the artist which proved providential.

Opposite: Belloni, who arrived young on the worksite, stayed for 24 years and died there (1964), hard at work until the end.

p.59: the Angel of Silence by Jean Larrivé is one of the most beautiful sculptures at Fourvière, and the plaster modello even more so.

The new generation of sculptors, introduced by Antoine Sainte-Marie Perrin, came up against a Commission which "favours the worst horrors," according to Larrivé, who won the competition to make the Chapel of the Visitation. He gave up that project to devote himself to the pulpit, causing more than a little trouble. The artist complained of having "to always fight against prejudices." His "Angel of Silence" (at the base of the north tower, west façade) is no doubt the masterpiece of Fourvière, admired for its restraint and a sort of inspired introspection. Following the untimely deaths of Larrivé and Antoine Sainte-Marie Perrin in 1928, Louis Bertola, winner of the Prix de Rome, finished the pulpit in 1930. Upon his return to Lyon in 1943, as a professor of Fine Arts, he was gravely disappointed at having been replaced at Fourvière by Belloni, a mere "technician." Joseph Belloni, who came to Lyon to decorate the Fair Hall, led the life of an ascetic on the work site. It took him 20 years (1943-1964) of hard-driving work to finish the north side and its virtuous women predating Mary, for example Judith and Esther representing Hope. In 1964, an angel at the base of the Tower of Justice (south tower) was left unfinished in honour of his work. It was not until the 21st century that some of Fourvière's major works were once again on display, thanks to the reorganisation of the museum, now one of the finest collections of sacred art in France.

With the sacristy hiding part of the south wall, Belloni brought together the themes of chastity and humility in an emblematic figure flanked by Susanna and the old men and the daughter of Jephte.

With the death of Antoine Sainte-Marie Perrin, the Commission dropped its commitment to the mysticism of the original designs. It also abandoned the theme of Maria d'Agréda, "Mary in the vision of God" planned for the tympanum of the great door, tied in with the theme of the cupolas. The bas-reliefs by Belloni, are more narrative and repre-

sent the most famous pilgrims and supporters of Fourvière. In addition to Pauline Jaricot, who had greatly suffered at the hands of the Commission, we see Frédéric Ozanam, Saint Vincent de Paul and the Curé d'Ars; on the right are the founders, including Fathers Jean-Claude Colin (Maristes), Marcellin Champagnat (Petits frères de Marie) and Antoine Chevrier (Prado). There are also the saints Thérèse Couderc (congregation of the Cénacle) and Claudine Thévenet (congregation of Jésus-Marie) and Élisabeth Rivet, Mother Superior of Notre-Dame de la Compassion, who died at Ravensbrück on 30 March 1945.

We owe these masterpieces by Larrivé (angel with sword, angel of silence, 1917-1920) to Antoine Sainte-Marie Perrin who imposed the young sculptor on a reticent commission. An unfinished angel by Belloni stands in commemoration of his work. He was succeeded by Darnas.

Opposite: stele of the rosary: designed by Bossan, sculpted by Fabisch, these little monuments, dedicated to the mysteries of the Rosary, were originally placed in the Rosaire garden to encourage pilgrims in their worship. They are now in the gardens facing the basilica.

p.63: roses not only symbolise the Virgin's virtues, they bear witness to the talent of Lyon's world-famed rose cultivators.

Opposite: under the trellises of roses, bronze plaques mark the 15 points of the rosary.

On this map, prior to the construction of the basilica, we can see the street Montée Nicolas de Lange, where the metal tower was later erected, and the Canons' grounds.

Fourvière is not meant for human eyes only; it was also conceived for the angels who see it from above. The visionary architect, who designed the vaulted ceilings with maniacal obsession, took care to place the Virgin Mary closer to God than to Man, but not without leaving us some hope of joining Mary one day in heaven.

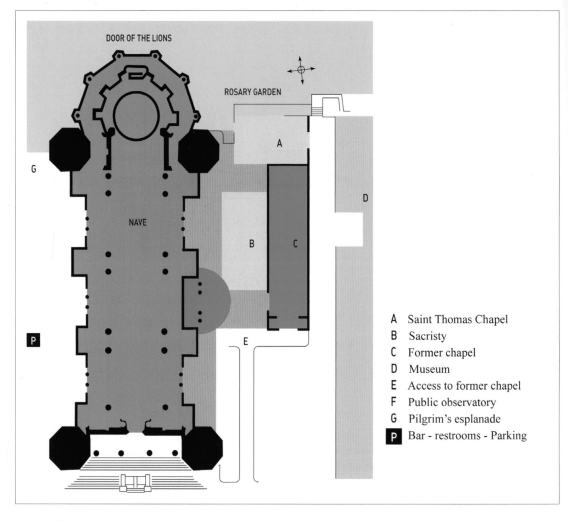

DOOR OF THE LIONS

ROSARY GARDEN

NAVE

A
B
C
D
E
G
P

A   Saint Thomas Chapel
B   Sacristy
C   Former chapel
D   Museum
E   Access to former chapel
F   Public observatory
G   Pilgrim's esplanade
P   Bar - restrooms - Parking

Bibliography

- HARDOUIN-FUGIER, Élisabeth, *Voir, revoir Fourvière*, Gabriel Lardant, Hauteville, 1988;

- BERTHOD, Bernard et HARDOUIN-FUGIER, Élisabeth, *Bossan et Armand-Calliat*, Lyon, Musée des Beaux-Arts, 1986;

- BERTHOD, Bernard, *1896-1996, Architecture et symboles, Fourvière a 100 ans*, Lyon, Musée de Fourvière, 1996;

- BERTHOD, Bernard, *1896-1996, La colline de Fourvière*, Sutton, 2001;

- GAMBIER, Gérald, *La merveilleuse histoire du 8 décembre à Lyon*, Châtillon-sur-Chalaronne, Éditions La Taillanderie, 2003;

Achevé d'imprimer en octobre 2006
Dépôt légal 3ᵉ trimestre 2006
Imprimé en U.E. par Beta Barcelone